JET ARABIC

A comprehensive,,small, effective Words & phrases guide.

(Spend some time & develop your Arabic Vocabulary)

A.M.K. SIDDIQUI

AL-KHAIR PUBLISHERS
HYDERABD-INDIA

Copyright ©

BOOK NAME::JET ARABIC
AUTHOR::A.M.K. SIDDIQUI
ISBN::978-81-923196-4-8
EDITION: FIRST

AL-KHAIR PUBLISHERS 2014
Powered by M/S Joudah Info-Lingo Tech Pvt.Ltd

#12-2-825/7
Ansar complex, 2nd floor
Mehdipatnam, Hyderabad-500028
Tel. 9140-6514-6277/ 9140-6634-6277
Email: info@alkhairpublishers.com
Website: www.alkhairpublishers.com

NOBLE INFOTECH
#204/B, 2nd Floor, Mustafa Towers,
Red Hills Road, Lakdikapul,
Hyderabad, Telangana 500004
Tel. 9140-4003-2472

And also available on:
Amazon.in / flipkart / shopclues
Fulilled by BIGeMART

Printed in India

All rights reserved.

No part of this publication may be reproduced, stored in a retrieval system, or transmitted, in any form or by any means, electronic, mechanical, photocopying, recording or otherwise, without the prior permission of the publishers.

بسم الله الرحيم

For every individual
who loves Arabic and
willing to speak
fluently.

Thanks to:

My Allah Almighty for his mercy on me.

The readers/students for their continuous love and support.

Each and every individual who has helped me in reaching this goal.

Especially **Mr.Abul Khiar Siddiqui (CEO - JILT PVT.LTD)** who irrespective of his busy schedule & commitments contributed & motivated to compress a dictionary in a different way.

Am thankful to **Mr.Mohd Nazeeruddin sahab** chairperson of ASRF who contributed and guided with his innovative ideas, and as well my dearest friends **Mr.Muhammad Ghazi Faheemuddin, Mr.Muhammad Muqtadir, Mr.Ateeq ur Rehaman Shariff Umri and Mr. Habeebuddin Umri** who contributed in proof-reading of this book. And dear brother **Mr.Abu Umar Siddiqui, Mr.Syed Basharath Mehdi, Mr.Syed Khaleelulah Hussaini** and **Mr.Abdur Raheem Siddiqui** who helped in publishing of this book to accomplish for the readers/learners as soon as possible.

A.M.K. SIDDIQUI
HYDERABAD - DECCAN

Preface

Today everyone is aware of Arabic language's importance, need and potential.

To promote the language many books have been published in various forms and everyday a new research is coming to light about the language. Indeed it's an unique language, based on the core principles of language.

In today's date many governmental, non-governmental and business institution are putting their efforts for Arabic language and the participants in the index list are increasing day by day .in fact it has been included in the syllabus of almost all universities in Europe and America. As the world is equipped with modern technology and many software has been innovated with the help of various programming languages and many apps have been built for android and windows smart phones to full fill the need of the hour. In the near past "MUDARRIS®" was introduced for the smart class, a bilingual (English-Urdu) Arabic learning software. Along with time & technology Arabic language is developing & getting promoted.

Where as many different books by many other authors are available in new forms &

ways and this book is one among of those efforts.

In this book very easy form has been used to compress necessary vocabulary in our day to day life.

All efforts have been made to gather almost 2000 words for the readers who are eager to grasp more often used vocabulary.

Some of the key features of the book are:

The capabilities of the readers have been considered.

Arabic words have been spelled in roman as well.

Besides these the classification is based on subjects or transactions of day to day life.

The whole & sole efforts were, to make it as simple as possible, if the readers have any better suggestions they are always welcome to write or contact Al-Khair publishers.

Well-wisher

A.M.K. SIDDIQUI
HYDERABAD – DECCAN

TIME

ENGLISH	ROMAN	العربية
Time	*zamaan*	زمان
Year	*Sana*	سنة
Week	*Usbu*	أسبوع
Day	*Yawm*	يوم
Hour	*Saah*	ساعة
Minute	*Daqiiqa*	دقيقة
Second	*Taanya*	ثانية
Sunday	*yoom al-aHad*	يوم الأحد
Monday	*yoom al-itnein*	يوم الاثنين
Tuesday	*yoom at-tulaataa'*	يوم الثلاثاء
Wednesday	*yoom al-arbiaa'*	يوم الأربعاء
Thursday	*yoom al-Khamiis*	يوم الخميس
Friday	*yoom al-juma*	يوم الجمعة
Saturday	*yoom as-sabt*	يوم السبت
Dawn	*Fajr*	فجر
Sunrise	*šuruuq aš-šams*	شروق الشمس
Morning	*SabaaH*	صباح
Noon	*Zuhr*	ظهر
Afternoon	*baad iZ-Zuhr*	بعد الظهر
Evening	*masaa'*	مساء

Sunset	ġuruub aš-šams	غروب الشمس
Midnight	muntaSaf al-leil	منتصف الليل
Night	Laiah	ليلة
One o'clock	as-saah al-waaHida	الساعة الواحدة
Before	Qabl	قبل
After	Baad	بعد
Then	Tumma	ثم
Until	Hatta	حتى
Now	al'aan	الآن
Day before yesterday	awwal ams	أول أمس
Yesterday	Ams	أمس
Last night	lailah ams	ليلة أمس
Today	al-yoom	اليوم
Tomorrow	Ġadan	غدا
Day after tomorrow	baad al-ġad	بعد الغد
Last (week)	(al-usbu) ul-maaDi	الأسبوع الماضي
Next (week)	(al-usbuu) ul-muqbil	الأسبوع المقبل
All day	Tuwaal al-yawm	طوال اليوم
Every day	kull yawm	كل يوم

Day after day	*yawman bad yawm*	يوما بعد يوم
Early	*Mubakkir*	مبكر
Late	*muta'aKhir*	متأخر
After a while	*bad qaliil*	بعد قليل

NUMBERS

ENGLISH	ROMAN	العربية
Zero	*Sifr*	صفر
One	*Wahid*	واحد
Two	*Ithnan*	إثنان
Three	*thalatha*	ثلاثة
Four	*arba'a*	أربعة
Five	*khamsa*	خمسة
Six	*Sitta*	ستة
Seven	*sab'a*	سبعة
Eight	*thamaaniya*	ثمانية
Nine	*tis'a*	تسعة
Ten	*'ashra*	عشرة
Eleven	*ihada 'ashar*	إحدى عشر
Twelve	*ithna 'ashar*	إثنا عشر
Thirteen	*thalatha 'ashar*	ثلاثة عشر
Fourteen	*arba'a 'ashar*	أربعة عشر
Fifteen	*khamsa 'ashar*	خمسة عشر
Sixteen	*sitta 'ashar*	ستة عشر
Seventeen	*sab'a 'ashar*	سبعة عشر
Eighteen	*thamaniya 'ashar*	ثمانية عشر
Nineteen	*tis'a 'ashar*	تسعة عشر

Twenty	*ishrun*	عشرون
Twenty one	*wahed wa-'ishrun*	واحد و عشرون
Twenty two	*ithnane wa-'ishrun*	إثنان وعشرون
Twenty-three	*thalatha wa-'ishrun*	ثلاثة و عشرون
Twenty-four	*arba'a wa-'ishrun*	أربعة و عشرون
Twenty five	*khamsa wa-'ishrun*	خمسة و عشرون
Twenty-six	*sitta wa-'ishrun*	ستة و عشرون
Twenty-seven	*sab'a wa-'ishrun*	سبعة وعشرون
Twenty-eight	*thamaniya wa-'ishrun*	ثمانية و عشرون
Twenty Nine	*tis'a wa-'ishrun*	تسعة و عشرون
Thirty	*thalathun*	ثلاثون
Forty	*arba'un*	أربعون
Fifty	*khamsun*	خمسون
Sixty	*Sittun*	ستون
Seventy	*sab'un*	سبعون
Eighty	*thamanun*	ثمانون
Ninety	*tis'un*	تسعون
Hundred	*mi'a*	مائة
Thousand	*alf*	ألف

MANKIND & KINDSHIP

ENGLISH	ROMAN	العربية
Age	umr	عمر
Bride	Aruus	عروس
Bridegroom	Ariis	عريس
Brother	Akh	أخ
Child	Tifl	طفل
Civilization	HaDaara	حضارة
Culture	Taqaafa	ثقافة
Divorce	Talaaq	طلاق
Engagement	KhuTuuba	خطوبة
Family	Aa'ila	عائلة
Father	Ab	أب
Fiancee	khaTiiba	خطيبة
Grandchild	Hafiid	حفيد
Grandfather	Jadd	جدّ
Grandmother	Jadda	جدة
Husband	Zawj	زوج
Individual	fard	فرد
Life	Hayaah	حياة
Man	Rajul	رجل
Marriage	zawaaj	زواج

Mother	*Umm*	أُمّ
Orphan	*Yatiim*	يتيم
People	*naas*	ناس
Person	*šakhS*	شخص
Relative	*Aqrab*	أقرب
Single,	*aazib*	أعزب
Sister	*uxt*	أخت
Society	*mujtama*	مجتمع
Son	*ibn*	إبن
Tradition	*Taqliid*	تقليد
Wife	*Zawja*	زوجة
Woman	*imra'a*	امرأة
Young boy	*fatan*	ىتً
Young girl	*fataah*	فتاة
Young man	*šaabb*	شاب
Young woman	*šaabba*	شابة
Younger	*Saġ iir*	صغير

WEATHER & NATURE

ENGLISH	ROMAN	العربية
Beach	*šaaTi'*	شاطئ
Branch	*fara*	فرع
Bush	*daġal*	دغل
Canal	*qanaah*	قناة
Cloud	*ġeima*	غيمة
Coast	*SaaHil*	ساحل
Cold	*baarid*	بارد
Continent	*qaarra*	قارّة
Degree	*daraja*	درجة
Desert	*SaHraa'*	صحراء
Dust	*turaab*	تراب
Earth	*arD*	أرض
Earthquake	*zilzaal*	زلزال
Environment	*bii'a*	بيئة
Autumm	*kariif*	خريف
Field	*Haql*	حقل
Fire	*naar*	نار
Flood	*fayaDaan*	فيضان
Flower	*zahra*	زهرة
Garden	*Hadiiqa*	حديقة

Gulf	*kaliij*	خليج
Hot	*Haar*	حار
Island	*jaziira*	جزيرة
Jungle	*ġaaba*	غابة
Lake	*buHeira*	بحيرة
Leaf	*waraq*	ورق
Lightning	*barq*	برق
Moon	*qamar*	قمر
Mountain	*jabal*	جبل
Nature	*aT-Tabiiah*	الطبيعة
Ocean	*muHiiT*	محيط
Planet	*kawkab*	كوكب
Plant	*nabaat*	نبات
Pond	*birka*	بركة
Port	*miinaa'*	ميناء
River	*nahr*	نهر
Root	*jadr*	جذر
Rose	*warda*	وردة
Sand	*raml*	رمل
Season	*faSl*	فصل
Sky	*samaa'*	سماء
Soil	*turba*	تربة

Spring	*rabie*	ربيع
Star	*najm*	نجم
Stone	*Hajar*	حجر
Summer	*Saif*	صيف
Sun	*šams*	شمس
Temperature	*darajat al-Haraara*	درجة الحرارة
The Red Sea	*al-baHr al-aHmar*	البحر الأحمر
Tree	*šajara*	شجرة
Valley	*waadi*	وادي
Waterfall	*šallaal*	شلال
Wave	*Mauj*	موج
Weather	*al-jaww*	الجوّ
Well	*bi'r*	بئر
Wind	*riiH*	ريح
Winter	*šitaa'*	شتاء
Wood	*kašab*	خشب
World	*Aalam*	عالم

EDUCATION

ENGLISH	ROMAN	العربية
Accounting	*almuhaasabah*	المحاسبة
Activity	*našaaT*	نشاط
Algebra	*aljabar*	الجبر
Architecture	*ali'maarah*	العمارة
Art	*fannun*	فن
Biology	*alahyaa*	الأحياء
Blackboard	*sabburah*	سبورة
Botany	*I'lmu nnabaat*	علم النبات
Business administration	*idaaratu alaa'maal*	إدارة الأعمال
Calculator	*aalatu haasibah*	آلة حاسبة
Certificate	*šahaada*	شهادة
Chalk	*Tabaashiir*	طباشير
Chemistry	*alkiimiyaa*	الكيمياء
Class	*Fasl*	فصل
Class period	*Hissatun*	حصّة
College	*kulliyya*	كلية
Computer science	*I'lmu lhaasoob*	علم الحاسوب
Curriculum	*manhaj*	منهج

Dance	*arraqs*	الرقص
Dentistry	*Tibbu linsaan*	طب الأسنان
Department	*qism*	قسم
Dictionary	*qaamus*	قاموس
Discussion	*munaaqaša*	مناقشة
Doctorate	*dactooraah*	دكتوراه
Economics	*aliqtisaad*	الإقتصاد
Elementary school	*al-madrasa l-ibtidaa'iyya*	المدرسة الإبتدائية
Encyclopedia	*mousua'h*	موسوعة
Engineering	*alhandasah*	الهندسة
Eraser	*mimhaat*	ممحاة
Exam	*imtiHaan*	إمتحان
Exercise	*tamriin*	تمرين
Fluency	*Talaaqah*	طلاقة
Geography	*aljugraafiyah*	الجغرافيا
Geology	*aljaiyalujiya*	الجيولوجيا
Grade	*Saff*	رف
Grammar	*qawaai'd*	قواعد
Higher education	*ad-diraasaat al-ulyaa*	الدراسات العليا
History	*attaariik*	التاريخ
Homework	*waajib*	واجب
Institute	*mahad*	معهد

Journalism	*asshaafah*	الصحافة
Kindergarten	*rawDat al-aTfaal*	روضة الأطفال
Language	*lugat*	لغة
Lecture	*muHaaDara*	محاضرة
Lesson	*dars*	درس
Linguistics	*allisaaniyaat*	اللسانيات
Literature	*aladab*	الأدب
Masters'	*majisteir*	ماجستير
Mathematic	*arriyaadiyaat*	الرياضيات
Music	*almousiqi*	الموسيقى
Notebook	*daftarun*	دفتر
Nursery school	*HaDaana*	حضانة
Optics	*albasariyaat*	البصريات
Paper	*waraqah*	ورقة
Pen	*qalam*	قلم
Pencil	*qalamu rasaas*	قلم رصاص
Pharmacy	*assaidaliyah*	الصيدلة
Philosophy	*alfalsafiyah*	الفلسفة
Physics	*alfiiziyah*	الفيزياء
Political science	*alu'loom assiyaasiyah*	العلوم السياسية
Presentation	*taqdiim*	تقديم

TECHNOLOGY

ENGLISH	ROMAN	العربية
CD	qurS maDġuuT	قرص مضغوط
Cell phone	Al-jawwal	الجوال
Computer	Haasuub	حاسوب
Copy	nuska	نسخة
CPU	waHdat al-muaalija al-markaziyya	وحدة المعالجة المركزية
Data	bayanaat	بيانات
Desktop wallpaper	Suura xalfiyyat aš-šaaša	صورة خلفية الشاشة
Digital	raqami	رقمي
DVD	qurS viidiyo raqami	قرص فيديو رقمي
Email	bariid elektroni	بريد الإلكتروني
File	malaff	ملف
Hard disk	qurS Sulb	قرص صلب
Hard drive	muHarrik Sulb	محرك صلب
Hardware	al-iataad aS-Sulb	العتاد الصلب
Key	zirr	زر
Keyboard	lawHat al-mafaatiiH	لوحة المفاتيح
Laptop	Haasuub maHmuul	حاسوب محمول

Link	*raabiT*	رابط
Memory card	*biTaaqat daakira*	بطاقة ذاكرة
Microphone	*laaqiT aS-Soot*	لاقط الصوت
Monitor	*šaaša*	شاشة
Motherboard	*lawHat umm*	لوحة أم
Mouse	*fa'ra*	فأرة
Multimedia	*wasaa'iT mutaddida*	وسائط متعددة
Operating system	*niZaam at-tašģiil*	نظام التشغيل
Password	*kalimat as-sirr*	كلمة السرّ
Printer	*Tabbaah*	طباعة
Processor	*muaalij*	معالج
Program	*barnaamaj*	برنامج
Programming language	*luģat al-barmaja*	لغة البرمجة
RAM	*daakirat al-wuSuul al-ašwaa'i*	ذاكرة الوصول العشوائي
Scanner	*maasiH Doo'i*	ماسح ضوئي
Screensaver	*HaafiZat aš-šaaša*	حافظة الشاشة
Search engine	*muHarrik-ul-baht*	محرك البحث
Server	*muzawwid*	مزود
SMS/	*risaala*	رسالة

Software	*barmajiyaat*	برمجيات
Speakers	*sammaat*	سماعات
The internet	*al-internet*	الإنترنت
Virtual	*wahmi*	وهمي
Website	*Mawqi al intarnet*	موقع الإنترنت
Wireless	*la silki*	لا سلكي

Professor	*ustaad*	أستاذ
Program	*barnaamaj*	برنامج
Pronunciation	*lafzun*	لفظ
Psychology	*I'lmu annafs*	علم النفس
Pupil	*tilmiid*	تلميذ
Recess	*ijaazah*	إجازة
Right,	*Sah*	صح
Scale	*misTarah*	مسطرة
Scholarship	*minhah*	منحة ، منح
School	*madrasa*	مدرسة
School subject	*maadda*	مادّة
Science	*I'lmun*	علم
Skill	*mahaarah*	مهارة
Sociology	*I'lmu alijtimaa'*	علم الإجتماع
Spelling	*tahajeah*	تهجئة
Statistics	*alihsaa*	الإحصاء
Student	*Taalib*	طالب
Studies	*diraasaat*	دراسات
Synonym	*muraadif*	مرادف
Teacher	*mudarris*	مدرّس
Test	*iktibaar*	إختبار
University	*jamia*	جامعة

BUSINESS

ENGLISH	ROMAN	العربية
Accounting	*Al muhaasaba*	المحاسبة
Accuracy	*Diqqa*	دقة
Alternative	*Albadeel*	البديل
Analysis	*Thaleel*	تحليل
Appropriate	*Mulaaima*	ملائمة
Authority	*Assultah*	السلطه
Bonds	*sanadaat*	سندات
Budget	*Miizaania*	ميزانية
Capital	*Ra sul maal*	رأس المال
Capitalism	*Ra asmalia*	رأس مالية
Cash	*Naqd*	نقد
Client	*A'meel\zaboon*	عميل/زبون
Commercial policy	*siyasah tijariyah*	سياسة تجارية
Competition	*munaafasah*	منافسة
Competitor	*munaafis*	منافس
Concepts	*mafaaheem*	مفاهيم
Conduct	*suluk*	سلوك
Consumer	*mustahlak*	مستهلك
Consumer's surplus	*faaiz-ul-mustahlik*	فائض المستهلك

English	Transliteration	Arabic
Consumption	*istahlaak*	إستهلاك
Contract	*aqad*	عقد
Cost	*taklafah*	تكلفة
Credit	*raseed*	رصيد
Crisis	*Azamaatul maliyah*	الأزمة المالية
Current account	*hisaabu jaarin*	حساب جاري
Debit	*dain*	دين
Deficit	*ala'juz*	العجز
Demand	*talab*	طلب
Department	*qismun*	قسم
Direct	*mubaashir*	مباشر
Direction	*ittijaah*	إتجاه
Distribution	*tauzi'*	تَوزيع
Domination	*saytarah*	سيطرة
Efficiency	*kafaa-atu*	كفائة
Efficient	*kafu*	كفوء
Employment	*Tashgeel*	تشغيل
Energy	*attaqah*	الطاقة
Equality	*masaawaat*	مساواة
Equilibrium	*Tawa azun*	توازن
Equity	*adaalah*	عدالة
Evaluation	*taqyeem*	تقييم

Excess	*faa-iz*	فائض
Exchange	*tabaadul*	تبادل
Exchange rate	*sa'ruassarf*	سعر الصرف
Expectation	*tawaqqau'*	توقع
Export	*tasdeer*	تصدير
External	*khaariji*	خارجي
Financing	*maali*	مالي
Foreign currency	*alu'mlatu alajnabiyyatu*	العمله الأجنبية
Hiring	*tauzeef*	توظيف
Import	*istiiraad*	استيراد
Income	*dakhal*	الدخل
Inflation	*tadakhum*	تضخم
Insurance sector	*qataau' attameen*	قطاع التأمين
Interest	*faaidah*	فائدة
Investment	*alistithmaar*	الإستثمار
Lease	*eejaar*	إيجار
Liabilities	*khusoom*	خصوم
Loan	*qarad*	قرض
Losses	*khasaair*	خسائر
Management	*alidaarah*	الإدارة
Manager	*mudeer*	مدير

Mismanagement	*suulidaarah*	سوء الإدارة
Monopoly	*ihtikaar*	إحتكار
Observation	*mulaahazah*	ملاحظة
Penniless	*muflis*	مفلس
Performance	*aladaau*	الأداء
Policies	*siyaasaat*	سياسات
Prediction	*tanbu*	تتبؤ
Productivity	*alintaajiyyah*	الإنتاجية
Profits	*alarbaah*	الأرباح
Project	*mashroo'*	مشروع
Purchases	*mushtariyaat*	مشتريات
Reputation	*shuhrah*	الشهره
Risk	*mukhaatarah*	مخاطره
Shareholder	*musaahim*	مساهم
Tax	*addareebah*	الضريبة
Trade	*tijaarah*	تجارة

Officer	*ZaabiT*	ضابط
Pilot	*Tayyaar*	طيار
Plumber	*sabbaak*	سباك
Policeman	*šurTi*	شرطي
Profession	*mihna*	مهنة
Qualifications	*mu'ahhilaat*	مؤهلات
Resume	*siira daatiyya*	سيرة ذاتية
Salary	*Raatibus-shahri*	راتب الشهري
Salesman	*baa'i*	بائع
Student	*Taalib*	طالب
Supervisor	*muraaqib*	مراقب
Tailor	*khayyaaT*	خياط
Teacher	*mudarris*	مدرس
Unemployment	*Bitala*	بطالة
Work	*Amal*	عمل
Worker	*Aamil*	عامل
Writer	*kaatib*	كاتب

WORK & MONEY

ENGLISH	ROMAN	العربية
Account	*Hisaab*	حساب
Accountant	*muHaasib*	محاسب
Assistant	*musaaid*	مساعد
Author	*mu'allif*	مؤلف
Baker	*kabbaaz*	خباز
Balance	*raSiid*	رصيد
Barber	*Hallaaq*	حلاق
Blacksmith	*Haddaad*	حداد
Boss	*mudiir*	مدير
Businessman	*rajul amaal*	رجل أعمال
Butcher	*jazzaar*	جزار
Carpenter	*najjaar*	نجار
Check	*šek*	شيك
Colleague	*zamiil*	زميل
Computer programmer	*mubarmij Haasuubaat*	مبرمج حاسوبات
Contractor	*muqaawil*	مقاول
Cook	*Tabbaak*	طباخ
Doctor	*Tabiib*	طبيب
Electrician	*kahrubaa'i*	كهربائي

English	Transliteration	Arabic
Employee	*muwaZZaf*	موظف
Employment	*tawZiif*	توظيف
Engineer	*muhandis*	مهندس
Experience	*kibra*	خبرة
Expert	*kabiir*	خبير
Farmer	*muzaari*	مزارع
Guard	*Haaris*	حارس
Inspector	*mufattiš*	مفتش
Inventor	*muktari*	مخترع
Jeweler	*jawharji*	جوهرى
Job	*waZiifa*	وظيفة
Job vacancy	*waZiifa šaaġira*	وظيفة شاغرة
Journalist	*SaHafi*	صحافي
Judge	*qaaDin*	قاضٍ
Lawyer	*muHaamin*	محامٍ
Librarian	*amiin maktaba*	أمين مكتبة
Maid	*kaddaama*	خدامة
Marketer	*musawwiq*	مسوق
Mechanic	*miikaaniki*	ميكانيكي
Merchant	*taajir*	تاجر
Money	*maal*	مال
Nurse	*mumarriD*	ممرض

RELIGION

ENGLISH	ROMAN	العربية
Religion	*diin*	دين
Islam	*al-islaam*	الإسلام
Alms-giving	*zakaah*	زكاة
Angel	*Malak*	ملك
Blessing	*baraka*	بركة
Buddhism	*al-buudiyya*	البوذية
Call to prayer	*adaan*	أذان
Chapter Of Qur'an	*suura*	سورة
Christian	*masiiHi*	مسيحي
Christianity	*al-masiiHiyya*	المسيحية
Church	*kaniisa*	كنيسة
Creed	*Aaqiida*	عقيدة
Evil	*šarr*	شر
Fasting	*Saum*	صوم
Fate	*qadr*	قدر
Forgiveness	*ġufraan*	غفران
Friday sermon	*kuTba*	خطبة
Good	*khair*	خير
Heaven	*al-janna*	الجنة
Hell	*an-naar*	النار

Hinduism	*al-hinduusiyya*	الهندوسية
Imam	*imaam*	إمام
Jainism	*al-jaaniyya*	الجانية
Jew	*yahuudi*	يهودي
Judaism	*al-yahuudiyya*	اليهودية
Judgement day	*Yaum ul-qiyaama*	يوم القيامة
Lord	*rabb*	رب
Mercy	*raHma*	رحمة
Minbar	*minbar*	منبر
Minor pilgrimage	*umrah*	عمرة
Miracle	*mujiza*	معجزة
Mosque	*jaami*	جامع
Muezzin	*mu'addin*	مؤذن
Muslim	*muslim*	مسلم
Pilgrimage to Mecca	*Hajj*	حج
Prayer	*Salaah*	صلاة
Prophet	*nabi*	نبي
Repentance	*tauba*	توبة
Resurrection	*qiyaama*	قيامة
Sacrifice	*DaHiya*	ضحية
Satan	*aš-šeiTaan*	الشيطان
Saviour	*mukalliS*	مخلّص

Secularism	*ilmaaniyya*	علمانية
Sikhism	*as-siikiyya*	السيخية
Sin	*kaTii'a*	خطيئة
Soul, spirit	*ruuH*	روح
Sufism	*aS-Suufiyya*	الصوفية
Temple	*mabad*	معبد
The Qur'an	*al-qur'aan*	القرآن
The Torah	*at-tauraah*	التوراة
Verse	*aaya*	آية
Witness of faith	*šahaada*	شهادة الايمان

ISLAM

ENGLISH	ROMAN	العربية
All Praises be to Allah the almighty	*Al hamdu lillha*	الحمد لله
Allah is the Greatest	*Allha hu akbar*	الله أكبر
Glory be to Allah	*Subhanallha*	سبحان الله
I ask Allah for forgiveness	*Astag firullah*	أستغفر الله
If Allah wills	*In sha allha*	إن شاء الله
In the name of Allah	*Bismilla*	بسم الله
inheritance	*Meeraas*	الميراث
Lawful	*Halaal*	حلال
May Allah be pleased with him	*Razi yallahu anhu*	رضي الله عنه
Peace Be Upon Him	*sallallaahu alaihi wa sallam*	صلى الله عليه و سلم
prayer	*Salaat*	صلاة
Prohibited	*Haraam*	حرام
Punishment	*Eqaab*	عقاب

BODY PARTS

ENGLISH	ROMAN	العربية
Abdomen	*baTn*	بطن
Arm	*diraa*	ذراع
Back	*Zahr*	ظهر
Beard	*liHya*	لحية
Beautiful	*jamiil*	جميل
Blood	*damm*	دمّ
Body	*jism*	جسم
Bone	*AaZm*	عظم
Brain	*dimaaġ*	دماغ
Chest	*Sadr*	صدر
Chin	*duqan*	ذقن
Dye	*Sibġa*	صبغة
Ear	*udun*	أذن
Eye	*Aein*	عين
Eyebrow	*Haajib*	حاجب
Face	*wajh*	وجه
Fat	*samiin*	سمين
Fingernail	*Zufr*	ظفر
Foot	*qadam*	قدم
Forehead	*jabiin*	جبين

English	Transliteration	Arabic
Gland	*ġudda*	غدة
Hair	*šar*	شَعر
Haircut	*qaSS aš-šar*	قصّ الشعر
Hand	*yad*	يد
Handsome	*wasiim*	وسيم
Head	*ra's*	رأس
Heart	*qalb*	قلب
Index finger	*sabbaaba*	سبابة
Kidney	*kulya*	كلية
Knee	*rukba*	ركبة
Knuckle, joint	*mafSil*	مفصل
Leg	*rijl*	رجل
Lip	*šafa*	شفة
Liver	*kabid*	كبد
Lung	*ri'a*	رئه
Middle finger	*wusTa*	وسطى
Mouth	*fam*	فم
Mustache	*šaarib*	شارب
Neck	*raqaba*	رقبة
Nose	*anf*	أنف
Palm	*raaHat*	راحة
Part	*ADw*	عضو

Pinky finger	*xinSir*	خنصر
Ring finger	*binSir*	بنصر
Saliva	*luaab*	لعاب
Short	*qaSiir*	قصير
Shoulder	*katif*	كتف
Skin	*jild*	جلد
Skull	*jumjuma*	جمجمة
Smell	*aš-šamm*	الشمّ
Stomach	*meda*	معدة
Tall	*Tawiil*	طويل
Taste	*at-tadawwuq*	التذوق
Thigh	*faxid*	فخذ
Thin	*naHiif*	نحيف
Throat	*Hanjara*	حنجرة
Thumb/big toe	*ibhaam*	إيهام
Tongue	*lisaan*	لسان
Tooth	*sinn*	سن
Touch	*al-lams*	اللمس
Ugly	*bašia*	بشع

AROUND THE HOUSE

ENGLISH	ROMAN	العربية
Balcony	*šurfa*	شرفة
Bathroom	*Hammaam*	حمّام
Bed	*sariir*	سرير
Bedroom	*ġurfat noom*	غرفة نوم
Blush	*aHmar al-kuduud*	أحمر الخدود
Bottle	*zujaaja*	زجاجة
Brush	*furšaah*	فرشاة
Candle	*šamah*	شمعة
Ceiling	*saqf*	سقف
Chair	*kursi*	كرسي
Coffee cup	*finjaan*	فنجان
Comb	*mušT*	مشط
Cup, glass	*kuub*	كوب
Desk	*maktab*	مكتب
Dining room	*ġurfah Ta'am*	غرفة طعام
Dining table	*maa'ida*	مائدة
Dish	*Tabaq*	طبق
Door	*baab*	باب
Door/handle	*miqbaD al-baab*	مقبض الباب
Drier	*jahaaz at-tanšiif*	جهاز التنشيف

English	Transliteration	Arabic
Electricity	*kahrabaa'*	كهرباء
Eyeliner	*zeit al-Kirwa*	زيت الخروع
Eyeshadow	*Zill*	ظلّ
Floor	*arDiyya*	أرضية
Foundation	*kriim al-asaas*	كريم الأساس
Fridge	*tallaaja*	ثلاجة
Furniture	*ataat*	أثاث
Gate	*bawwaaba*	بوّابة
Hammer	*miTraqa*	مطرقة
Iron	*mikwaah*	مكواة
Iron	*Hadiid*	حديد
Jug	*ibriiq*	إيريق
Key	*miftaaH*	مفتاح
Kitchen	*maTbaq*	مطبخ
Knife	*sikkiin*	سكّين
Lamp	*miSbaaH*	مصباح
Light	*nuur*	نور
Lipstick	*aHmar aš-šifaah*	أحمر الشفاة
Makeup	*maakiyaaž*	ماكياج
Mat	*mimsaHa*	ممسحة
Mirror	*miraah*	مرآة
Nail	*mismaar*	مسمار

English	Transliteration	Arabic
Neighbor	*jaar*	جار
Paint	*dihaan*	دهان
Pipe	*maasuura*	ماسورة
Powder	*buudra*	بودرة
Remote control	*Haakim an bud*	حاكم عن بعد
Roof	*saTH*	سطح
Room	*ġurfa*	غرفة
Scissors	*miqaSS*	مقصّ
Screw	*burġi*	برغي
Shampoo	*šaambuu*	شامبو
Sink	*maġsala*	مغسلة
Soap	*Sabuun(a)*	صابون
Sofa	*ariika*	أريكة
Spoon	*milaqa*	ملعقة
Stairs	*salaalim*	سلالم
Steel	*Sulb*	بلد
Table	*Taawula*	طاولة
Tablecloth	*ġiTaa' aT-Taawula*	غطاء الطاولة
Telephone	*tilifoon*	تلفون
Television	*televizyoon*	تلفزيون
To rent	*ajjara*	أجر
Toilet	*doorat al-miyaah*	دورة مياة

Toilet paper	*waraq tuwalitt*	ورق تواليت
Tool	*adaah*	أداة
Toothbrush	*furšaat asnaan*	فرشاة أسنان
Toothpaste	*majuun asnaan*	معجون أسنان
Towel	*minšafa*	منشفة
Wall	*jidaar*	جدار
Washing machine	*ġassaala*	غسّالة
Window	*šubbaak*	شبّاك

CLOTHES

ENGLISH	ROMAN	العربية
Bangle	*siwaar*	سوار
Belt	*Hizaam*	حزام
Button	*zirr*	زرّ
Clothes	*malaabis*	ملابس
Coat	*miTaf*	معطف
Collar	*qubba*	قبّة
Cotton	*quTun*	قطن
Diamond	*maas*	ماس
Gold	*dahab*	ذهب
Jacket	*sutratu*	سترة
Jewel	*jawhara*	جوهرة
Pants	*banTaloon*	بنطلون
Pearls	*lu'lu'*	لؤلؤ
Pocket	*jaib*	جيب
Purse	*šanTa*	شنطة
Ring	*kaatam*	خاتم
Scarf	*wišaaH*	وشاح
Shirt	*qamiiS*	قميص
Shoe	*Hidaa'*	حذاء
Silver	*fiDDa*	فضّة

Slipper	*kuff*	خفّ
Sock	*jawrab*	جورب
Suit	*badla*	بدلة
Thread	*khaiT*	خيط
Tie	*rabTa unuq*	ربطة عنق
Umbrella	*miZalla*	مظلّة
Wallet	*miHfaZa*	محفظة
Wristwatch	*saath yad*	ساعة يد

FOOD

ENGLISH	ROMAN	العربية
Alcohol	*Khamr*	خمر
Almonds	*looz*	لوز
Apple	*tuffaaH*	تفّاح
Apricot	*mišmiš*	مشمش
Banana	*mooz*	موز
Box	*Sunduuq*	صندوق
Breakfast	*faTuur*	فطور
Cabbage	*krumb*	كرمب
Carrot	*jazar*	جزر
Coconut	*jooz al-hind*	جوز الهند
Coffee	*qahwa*	قهوة
Dates	*tamar*	تمر
Dinner	*Aašaa'*	عشاء
Drink	*mašruub*	مشروب
Eggplant	*baadinjaan*	باذنجان
Food	*Taam*	طعام
Fruit	*faakiha*	فاكهة
Full (from eating)	*šabaan*	شبعان
Grape	*inab*	عنب

Hungry	*jaa'ie*	جائع
Juice	*AaSiir*	عصير
Lemon	*laymuun*	ليمون
Lunch	*ġadaa'*	غداء
Mango	*mango*	مانجو
Milk	*Haliib*	حليب
Okra	*baamiya*	بامية
Orange	*burtuqaal*	برتقال
Piece	*qitTah*	قطعة
Pineapple	*ananaas*	اناناس
Pomegranate	*rummaan*	رمّان
Recipe	*waSfa*	وصفة
Restaurant	*maTam*	مطعم
Slice	*šariiHa*	شريحة
Tea	*šaay*	شاي
Thirsty	*aTšaan*	عطشان
Vegetables	*KhaDrawaat*	خضراوات
Waiter	*naadil*	نادل
Water	*maa'*	ماء

PULSES – CEREALS

ENGLISH	ROMAN	العربية
Black	*aswad*	أسود
Blue	*azraq*	أزرق
Bright	*barraaq*	براق
Brown	*asmar*	أسمر
Color	*loun*	لون
Colored	*mulawwan*	ملوّن
Cream	*aSfar šaaHib*	أصفر شاحب
Dark	*ġaamiq*	غامق
Golden	*dahabi*	ذهبي
Green	*AkhaDar*	أخضر
Grey	*ramaadi*	رمادي
Maroon	*kastanaa'i*	كستنائي
Orange	*burtuqaali*	برتقالي
Pink	*zahri*	زهري
Purple	*urjuwaani*	أرجواني
Red	*aHmar*	أحمر
Rose-colored	*wardi*	وردي
Semolina	*Sameed*	سميد
Sesame	*Simsim*	سمسم
Shiny	*laamia*	لامع

Silver	*fiDDi*	فضي
White	*aswad*	أسود
Yellow	*azraq*	أزرق

SPICES

ENGLISH	ROMAN	العربية
Asafoetida	*hiltiit*	حلتيت
Black pepper	*Alfilfilul aswad*	الفلفل الأسود
Brown cardamom	*Bunni alheel*	بني الهيل
Carom seeds / thyme	*Bazur karratul hamra*	بذور الكرة الحمراء
Cumin	*Kamoon*	كمون
Green cardamom	*Heel ul aqzar*	الهيل الأخضر
Mace	*Soljaan*	صولجان
Nutmeg	*Jouwzu attayyib*	جوزة الطيب
Star anise	*Njmatul yansun*	نجمة اليانسون

MEDICINE

ENGLISH	ROMAN	العربية
Allergy	*Hassaasiyya*	حسّاسية
Ambulance	*isaaf*	إسعاف
Band-aid	*plastar*	بلاستر
Blind	*aAma*	أعمى
Blood pressure	*DaġT ad-damm*	ضغط الدم
Clinic	*Eiyaada*	عيادة
Coma	*ġaibuuba*	غيبوبة
cough	*sualah*	سعلة
Deaf	*aTraš*	أطرش
Dentist	*Tabiib al-asnaan*	طبيب الأسنان
Diabetes	*maraD as-sukkar*	مرض السكّر
Disease	*maraD*	مرض
Doctor	*Tabiib*	طبيب
Fever	*Humma*	حمّى
Headache	*Sudaa*	صداع
Health	*SiHHa*	صحة
Heart attack	*azma qalbiyya*	أزمة قلبية
Hospital	*mustašfa*	مستشفى
Kidney stone	*HaSwa*	حصوة
Leprosy	*judaam*	جذام

Medicine	*aT-Tibb*	الطبّ
Medicine	*dawaa'*	دواء
Nurse	*mumarriD*	ممرّض
Nursing	*at-tamriiD*	التمريض
Operation	*Aamaliyya*	عملية
Pain	*waja*	وجع
Paralyzed	*mašluul*	مشلول
Patient	*mariiD*	مريض
Pharmacy	*Saidaliyya*	صيدلية
Sick, ill	*mariid*	مريض
sneeze	*aTsa*	عطسة
Stethoscope	*sammaaa*	سمّاعة
Strong	*qawi*	قوي

COUNTRY

ENGLISH	ROMAN	العربية
Africa	*afriiqiya*	أفريقيا
Algeria	*al-jazaa'ir*	الجزائر
Algiers	*al-jiiriya*	الجيريا
Asia	*aasiya*	أسيا
Australia	*usturaaliya*	أستراليا
Cairo	*al-qaahira*	القاهرة
Capital	*AaSima*	عاصمة
China	*aS-Siin*	الصين
Damascus	*dimašq*	دمشق
District	*Hayy*	حيّ
Egypt	*miSr*	مصر
England	*inglitira*	إنجلترا
Europe	*urubba*	أوروبا
Germany	*almaaniya*	ألمانيا
Greece	*yuunaan*	يونان
Homeland	*waTan*	وطن
India	*al-hind*	الهند
Israel	*israa'iil*	إسرائيل
Japan	*yaabaan*	يابان
Jordan	*al-'urdunn*	الأردن

Libya	*liibiyaa*	ليبيا
Location,	*mawqi*	موقع
Madina	*al-madiin a l-munawwara*	المدينة المنوّرة
Map	*KhariiTa*	خريطة
Marrakesh	*marraakeš*	مراكش
Mecca	*makka (al-mukarrama)*	مكّة (المكرّمة)
Palestine	*filasTiin*	فلسطين
Place	*makaan*	مكان
Region	*minTaqa*	منطقة
Syria	*suuriya*	سوريا
UK	*al-mamlaka al-muttaHida*	المملكة المتحدة
US	*amriika*	أُمريكا
Village	*qaryah*	قرية

CITY

ENGLISH	ROMAN	العربية
Accident	*Haadita*	حادثة
Airport	*maTaar*	مطار
Apartment	*šuqqa*	شقة
ATM	*Sarraaf aali*	صرّاف آلي
Bakery	*maKhbaz*	مخبز
Bench	*maqad*	مقعد
Bicycle	*darraaja*	درّاجة
Boat	*markab*	مركب
Bridge	*jisr*	جسر
Building	*imaara*	عمارة
Bus	*Haafila*	حافلة
Cafe	*maqha*	مقهى
Car	*sayyaara*	سيارة
Center	*markaz*	مركز
City	*madiina*	مدينة
Clinic	*iyaada*	عيادة
Club	*naadii*	نادي
Company	*šarika*	شركة
Crowdedness	*izdiHaam*	ازدحام
Driver	*saa'iq*	سائق

English	Transliteration	Arabic
Driving license	*rukhSatu qiyaada*	رخصة قيادة
Grocery shop	*baqqaala*	بقالة
Helicopter	*marwaHiyya*	مروحية
Hospital	*mustašfa*	مستشفى
Hotel	*funduq*	فندق
House	*bait*	بيت
Insurance	*ta'miin*	تأمين
Library	*maktaba*	مكتبة
Mosque	*masjid*	مسجد
Motorcycle	*darraaja naariyya*	درّاجة نارية
Museum	*matHaf*	متحف
Noise	*Dajja*	ضجّة
Palace	*qaSr*	قصر
Passport	*jawaaz*	جواز
Pharmacy	*Saydaliyya*	صيدلية
Plane	*Taa'ira*	طائرة
Platform	*raSiif*	رصيف
Police station	*qism aš-šorTa*	قسم الشرطة
Post office	*maktab al-bariid*	مكتب البريد
Queue	*Taabuur*	طابور
Real estate	*Iqaar*	عقار
Restaurant	*maTam*	مطعم

English	Transliteration	Arabic
Road	*Tariiq*	طريق
School	*madrasa*	مدرسة
Ship	*safiina*	سفينة
Shop	*maHall*	محلّ
Station	*maHaTTa*	محطة
Street	*šaari*	شارع
Swimming pool	*Hammaam as-sibaaHa*	حمّام السباحة
Taxi	*taksi*	تاكسي
Temple	*maabad*	معبد
Tourism	*siyaaHa*	سياحة
Traffic	*muruur*	مرور
Traffic signals	*išaaraat al-muruur*	إشارات المرور
Traffic signs	*Aalaamaat al-muruur*	علامات المرور
Train	*qiTaar*	قطار
trip	*riHla*	رحلة
Truck	*šaaHina*	شاحنة
University	*jaamia*	جامعة
Visa	*ta'šiira*	تأشيرة
Zoo	*Hadiiqat al-Hayawaan*	حديقة الحيوان

GOVERNMENT & POLITICS

ENGLISH	ROMAN	العربية
Against	*Didd*	ضد
Agency	*wakaala*	وكالة
Ambassador	*safiir*	سفير
Authority	*sulTa*	سلطة
Capitalism	*ra'smaaliyya*	رأسمالية
Citizen	*muwaaTin*	مواطن
Committee	*lajna*	لجنة
Communism	*šuyuiyya*	شيوعية
Constitution	*dustuur*	دستور
Council	*majlis*	مجلس
Councillor	*mustašaar*	مستشار
Country	*dawla*	دولة
Delegation	*wafd*	وفد
Democracy	*diimoqraaTiyya*	ديموقراطية
Deputy	*wakiil*	وكيل
Deputy	*naa'ib*	نائب
Embassy	*safaara*	سفارة
Empire	*imbraaTuuriyya*	امبراطورية
Equality	*musaawaah*	مساواة
Executive	*tanfiidi*	تنفيذي

Federal government	*Hukuuma ittiHaadiyya*	حكومة إتحادية
Freedom	*Hurriyya*	حرية
Government	*Hukuuma*	حكومة
Governor	*Haakim*	حاكم
Half	*naSf*	نصف
Human rights	*Huquuq ul-insaan*	حقوق الإنسان
Immigrant	*muhaajir*	مهاجر
Institution	*mu'assasa*	مؤسسة
Issue	*qaDiyya*	قضية
Judicial	*qaDaa'i*	قضائي
King	*malik*	ملك
Kingdom	*mamlaka*	مملكة
Law	*qaanuun*	قانون
Leader	*zaiim*	زعيم
Legislative	*tašrie*	تشريعي
Local government	*al-Hukuuma al-maHaliyya*	الحكومة المحلية
Majority	*aġlabiyya*	أغلبية
Mayor	*umda*	عمدة
Minister	*waziir*	وزير
Ministry of defense	*wizaarat ad-difaa*	وزارة الدفاع

English	Transliteration	Arabic
Ministry of foreign affairs	*wizaarat al-Khaarijiyya*	وزارة الخارجية
Ministry of health	*wizaarat aS-SiHHa*	وزارة الصحة
Morals	*akhlaaq*	أخلاق
Movement	*Haraka*	حركة
Nation	*waTan*	وطن
Nationalism	*qawmiyya*	قومية
Official	*Rasmi*	رسمي
Oppression	*Zulm*	ظلم
Organization	*munaZZama*	منظمة
Parliament	*barlamaan*	برلمان
Party	*Hizb*	حزب
Peace	*salaam*	سلام
Percentage	*nisba*	نسبة
Policy	*siyaasa*	سياسة
Political	*siyaasi*	سياسي
Politics	*as-siyaasa*	السياسة
Population	*Adad sukkaan*	عدد سكان
Position	*manSab*	منصب
President	*ra'iis*	رئيس
Prime minister	*ra'iis al-wuzaraa'*	رئيس الوزراء
Prince	*amiir*	أمير

Protection	*Himaaya*	حماية
Reform	*iSlaaH*	إصلاح
Republic	*jumhuuriyya*	جمهورية
Resolution	*qaraar*	قرار
Result	*natiija*	نتيجة
Right	*Haqq*	حق
Safety	*salaama*	سلامة
Secretary general	*al-amiin al-Aamm*	الأمين العام
Security	*amn*	أمن
Session	*jalsa*	جلسة
Slavery	*ubuudiyya*	عبودية
Socialism	*ištiraakiyya*	إشتراكية
Stability	*istiqraar*	إستقرار
Standard	*meyaar*	معيار
The General Assembly	*al-jamaiyya al-Aamma*	الجمعية العامة
The Supreme Court	*al-maHkama al-ulya*	المحكمة العليا
The United Nations	*al-umam al-muttaHida*	الأمم المتحدة
Theft	*sariqa*	سرقة
Torture	*tadiib*	تعذيب

Unity	*waHda*	وحدة
Women's rights	*Huquuq ul-mar'a*	حقوق المرأة
World bank	*al-bank ad-dawli*	البنك الدولي

ENGLISH	ROMAN	العربية
A waste of time	*Khasaarat ul-waqt*	خسارة الوقت
Actor	*mumattil*	ممثّل
After a while	*baad qaliil*	بعد قليل
Art	*fann*	فن
Artist	*fannaan*	فنان
Astonishing	*mudhil*	مذهل
Attractive	*jaddaab*	جذاب
Author	*mu'allif*	مؤلف
Book	*kitaab*	كتاب
Breaking news	*aKhbaar Aajila*	أخبار عاجلة
Camera	*kamira*	كاميرا
Cartoon	*kartuun*	كرتون
Channel	*qanaah*	قناة
Comedy	*komedy*	كوميدي
Critic	*naaqid*	ناقد
Drama	*draama*	دراما
Drawing	*rasm*	رسم
Editing	*taHriir*	تحرير
Editor	*ra'iis taHriir*	رئيس تحرير

Enjoyable	*mumatti*	ممتع
Entertaining	*musallin*	مسلٍ
Excellent	*raa'i*	رائع
Famous	*mašhuur*	مشهور
Fun	*maraH*	مرح
Funny	*muDHik*	مضحك
Great	*mumtaaz*	ممتاز
Historical	*taariiKi*	تاريخي
Horror	*rub*	رعب
Journalism,	*SaHaafa*	صحافة
Journalist	*Sahafi*	صحافي
Line	*saTr*	سطر
Live	*mubaašir*	مباشر
Magazine	*majalla*	مجلة
Movie	*film*	فيلم
Negative	*salbi*	سلبي
Newspaper	*jariida*	جريدة
Page	*SafHa*	صفحة
Painter	*rassaam*	رسام
Paragraph	*fiqra*	فقرة
Passage	*naSS*	نص
Performance	*adaa'*	أداء

Photographer	*muSawwir*	مصور
Photography	*taSwiir*	تصوير
Picture	*Suura*	صورة
Poem	*qaSiida*	قصيدة
Poetry	*šir*	شعر
Positive	*iijaabi*	إيجابي
Poster	*mulSaq*	ملصق
Promotion	*tarwiij*	ترويج
Report	*taqriir*	تقرير
Review	*muraajah*	مراجعة
Screen	*šaaša*	شاشة
Sentence	*jumla*	جملة
Series	*silsila*	سلسلة
Star	*najm*	نجم
Statue	*timtaal*	تمثال
Ticket	*tadkira*	تذكرة
Unique	*fariid*	فريد
Voice	*Soot*	صوت
War	*Harb*	حرب
Word	*kalima*	كلمة
Writer	*Kaatib*	كاتب

CRIME & PUNISHMENT

ENGLISH	*ROMAN*	العربية
Bail	*kafaala*	كفالة
Case	*qaDiyya*	قضية
Court	*maHkama*	محكمة
Crime	*jariima*	جريمة
Criminal	*mujrim*	مجرم
Defense	*difa*	دفاع
Eyewitness	*šaahid Aiyaan*	شاهد عيان
Fine	*ġaraama*	غرامة
Guilty	*mudnib*	مذنب
Hanging	*šanq*	شنق
Illegal	*ġeir qaanuuni*	غير قانوني
Innocent	*bari'*	برئ
Murderer	*saffaaH*	سفاح
Prison	*sijn*	سجن
Prisoner	*asiir*	أسير
Proof	*daliil*	دليل
Prosecution	*iddia'*	إدعاء
Punishment	*iqaab*	عقاب
Rape	*iġtiSaab*	إغتصاب
Robbery	*nahb*	نهب

Smuggling	*tahriib*	تهريب
Trial	*muHaakama*	محاكمة
Victim	*DaHiyya*	ضحية
Warrant	*mudakkirat tawqiif*	مذكرة توقيف
Witness	*šaahid*	شاهد

EMOTIONS & PERSONALITY

ENGLISH	ROMAN	العربية
Afraid	*Khaa'if*	خائف
Angry	*ġaaDib*	غاضب
Bashful	*khajuul*	خجول
Busy	*mašġuul*	مشغول
Comfortable	*murtaaH*	مرتاح
Confused	*Haa'ir*	حائر
Content	*raaDi*	راضي
Delighted	*masruur*	مسرور
Emotion	*AaTif*	عاطف
Envious	*Hasuud*	حسود
Feeling	*šaAr*	شعر
Glad,	*farHaan*	فرحان
Happy	*saiid*	سعيد
Hate	*karaahiyya*	كراهية
Jealous	*ġayuur*	غيور
Love	*Hubb*	حبّ
Miserable	*miskiin*	مسكين
Naughty	*šaqi*	شقي
Passion	*Shagaf*	شغف
Personality	*šakhSiyya*	شخصية

Proud	*fakhuur*	فخور
Regretful	*naadim*	نادم
Sad	*Haziin*	حزين
Sensitive	*Hassaas*	حساس
Tear	*dam*	دمع
Tense	*mutawattir*	متوتر
Tired	*mutib*	متعب
Worries	*hamm*	هم
Afraid	*Khaa'if*	خائف

DIRECTIONS

ENGLISH	ROMAN	العربية
Above	*fooqa*	فوق
Area	*misaaHa*	مساحة
Behind	*waraa'*	وراء
Below	*taHt*	تحت
Between	*beina*	بين
Compass	*boSla*	بوصلة
Direction	*ittijaah*	إتجاة
Distance	*masaafa*	مسافة
East	*šarq*	شرق
Far	*baiid*	بعيد
Height	*irtifaa*	إرتفاع
Here	*huna*	هنا
In front of	*amaam*	أمام
Inside	*daakhil*	داخل
Left	*yasaar*	يسار
Length	*Tuul*	طول
Near	*qariib min*	قريب
Next to	*bijaanib*	بجانب
North	*šimaal*	شمال
Opposite	*muqaabil*	مقابل

Outside	*kharij*	خارج
Right	*yamiin*	يمين
South	*januub*	جنوب
There	*hunaaka*	هناك
West	*ġarb*	غرب
Width	*AarD*	عرض

WAR

ENGLISH	ROMAN	العربية
Air force	*quwwaat jawwiyya*	قوات جوية
Atomic bomb	*qunbula durriyya*	قنبلة ذرية
Battle	*maraka*	معركة
Bloodshed	*safk ad-dimaa'*	سفك الدماء
Bomb	*qunbula*	قنبلة
Brigadier	*Aamiid*	عميد
Bullet	*raSaaSa*	رصاصة
Chemical weapons	*asliHa kiimaawiyya*	أسلحة كيماوية
Colonel	*Aaqiid*	عقيد
Commander in chief	*al-qaa'id al-ala*	القائد الأعلى
Defeat	*haziima*	هزيمة
Defense	*difaa*	دفاع
Enemy	*Aduuww*	عدو
Forces	*quwwaat*	قوات
General	*liwaa'*	لواء
Heavy	*taqiil*	ثقيل
Innocent	*bari'*	بريء
Killed,	*qatiil*	قتيل

Light	*Khafiif*	خفيف
Loss	*kasaara*	خسارة
Major	*raa'id*	رائد
Martyr	*šahiid*	شهيد
Navy	*al-baHariyya*	البحرية
Nuclear weapons	*asliHa nawawiyya*	أسلحة نووية
Officer	*DaabiT*	ضابط
Revolution	*thawra*	ثورة
Soldier	*jundi*	جندي
Sword	*saife*	سيف
Treaty	*muaahada*	معاهدة
Victory	*Najaah*	نجاح
Violence	*Aunf*	عنف
War	*Harb*	حرب

ANIMALS

ENGLISH	ROMAN	العربية
Spider	*Aankabuut*	عنكبوت
Scorpion	*Aaqraba*	عقربة
Elephant	*fiil*	فيل
Sheep	*ġanam*	غنم
Horse	*HiSaan*	حصان
Wing	*jinaaH*	جناح
Rabbit	*arnab*	أرنب
Fish	*samak*	سمك
Parrot	*babġaa'*	ببغاء
Mosquito	*bauDah*	بعوضة
Cow	*baqara*	بقرة
Duck	*baTatah*	بطة
Hippopotamus	*barniiq*	برنيق
Frog	*Difdia*	ضفدع
Hen	*dajaajah*	دجاجة
Worm	*duudh*	دودة
Rooster	*diik*	ديك
Tail	*deil*	ذيل
Rat	*fa'r*	فأر
Butterfly	*faraaš*	فراشة

Crow	*ġuraab*	غراب
Deer	*ġazaal*	غزال
Donkey	*Himaar*	حمار
Pigeon	*Hamaamah*	حمامة
Insect	*Hašara*	حشرة
Animal	*Hayawaan*	حيوان
Whale	*Huut*	حوت
Buffalo	*jaamuus*	جاموس
Camel	*jamal*	جمل
Dog	*kalb*	كلب
Goat	*maaiz*	ماعز
Bee	*naHlh*	نحلة
Ant	*namlah*	نملة
Tiger	*namir*	نمر
Eagle	*nasr*	نسر
Cat	*qiTTa*	قطّة
Monkey	*qird*	قرد
Shark	*qirš*	قرش
Feather	*riišah*	ريشة
Bird	*Taa'ir*	طائر
Crocodile	*timsaaH*	تمساح
Peacock	*Taawuus*	طاووس

Arabic Verbs

Basic Tenses in Arabic

There are only two basic tenses in Arabic:

The past - The present

• The past stem is formed from the three root letters, Like
شرب (shariba) it mean <he drank>
• The present stem is formed from the three root letters and
adding the Prefixes of present tenses like.
yashrabu (he drinks or he will drink)

1 Past	2 Present	3 Root
فعل	يفعل	فعلاً
He work	He works / he will work	To work

Snake	*thubaan*	ثعبان
Bull, ox	*thour*	ثور
Lion	*asad*	أسد
Pig	*Khanziir*	خنزير
Lamb	*Kharuuf*	خروف
Dove	*yamaamah*	يمامة
Fly	*dubaabah*	ذبابة
Dolphin	*duKhas*	دخس
Cockroach	*SurSuur*	صرصور

BASIC VERBS

ENGLISH	ROMAN		العربية
To advise	*Nasaha*	1 -Past	نصح
	yanshu	2 Present	ينصح
	insah	3 Root	إنصاح
To arrive	*waSala*		وصل
	yaSilu		يصل
	wuSuul		وصول
To ask	*sa'ala*		سأل
	yas'alu		يسأل
	su'aal		سؤال
To be	*kaana*		كان
	yakuunu		يكون
	kaun		كون
To be able to do	*Qadara*		قدر
	yaqdiru		يقدر
	qudra		قدرة
To be able to do	*istaTaa*		إستطاع
	yastaTii		يستطيع
	istiTaah		استطاعة

To be born	*wulida*	وُلِد
	yuuladu	يُولد
	wilaada	ولادة
To become	*aSbaHa*	أصبح
	yuSbiHu	يصبح
	iSbaaH	اصباح
To begin	*bada'a*	بدأ
	yabda'u	يبدأ
	bad'	بدء
To believe	*itaqada*	إعتقد
	yataqidu	يعتقد
	itiqaad	اعتقاد
To bring	*aHDara*	أحضر
	yuHDiru	يحضر
	iHDaar	احضار
To buy	*Ištara*	اشترى
	yaštari	يشتري
	širaa'	شراء
To carry	*Hamala*	حمل
	yaHmilu	يحمل
	Haml	حمل

To change	*ġayyara*	غيّر
	yuġayyiru	يغيّر
	taġyiir	تغيير
To clean	*naZZafa*	نظّف
	yunaZZifu	ينظّف
	tanZiif	تتنظيف
To close	*ġalaqa*	قل
	yaġliqu	يغلق
	ġalq	قلغ
To come	*jaa'a*	جاء
	yajii'u	يجئ
	jii'a	جيئة
To complain	*šaka*	شكى
	yašku	يشكو
	šakwa	شكوى
To cook	*Tabakha*	طبخ
	yaTbukhu	يطبخ
	Tabkh	طبخ
To count	*adda*	عدّ
	yauddu	يعدّ
	Add	عدّ

To describe	*waSafa*	وصف
	yaSifu	يصف
	waSf	وصف
To die	*Maata*	مات
	yamuutu	يموت
	maut	موت
To do	*Fa'ala*	فعل
	yafalu	يفعل
	fial	فعل
To drink	*Šariba*	شرب
	yašrabu	يشرب
	šurb	شرب
To eat	*Akala*	أكل
	yaa'kulu	يأكل
	akl	أكل
To end	*Intaha*	إنتهى
	yantahi	ينتهي
	intihaa'	إنتهاء
To enter	*Dakhala*	دخل
	yadkhulu	يدخل
	Dukhul	دخول

To fail	*Fašila*	فشِل
	yafšalu	يفشِل
	fašal	فشَل
To fall	*waqaa*	وقع
	yaqau	يقع
	wuqu	وقوع
To find	*Wajada*	وجد
	yajidu	يجد
	wujuud	وجود
To finish	*KhallaSa*	خلّص
	yuKhalliSu	يخلّص
	taKhliiS	تخليص
To forget	*Nasiya*	نسِي
	yansaa	ينسى
	nasi	نسي
To get up	*Qaama*	قام
	yaquumu	يقوم
	qiyaam	قيام
To give	*aaTa*	أعطى
	yuTi	يعطي
	iTaa'	اعطاء

To go to	*Dahaba*	ذهب
	yadhabu	يذهب
	dahaab	ذهاب
To go down	*Nazala*	نزل
	yanzilu	ينزل
	nuzuul	نزول
To go out	*Kharaja*	خرج
	yaKhruju	يخرج
	Khuruuj	خروج
To go up	*Talaa*	طلع
	yaTlau	يطلع
	Tulu	طلوع
To happen	*Hadata*	حدث
	yaHdutu	يحدث
	Huduut	حدوث
To hate	*Kariha*	كره
	yakrahu	يكره
	karh	كره
To hear	*samia*	سمع
	yasmau	يسمع
	Samaaa	سماع

To know	*arafa*	عرف
	yarifu	يعرف
	marifa	معرفة
To learn	*taallama*	تعلّم
	yataallamu	يتعلّم
	taallum	تعلّم
To leave	*Ġaadara*	غادر
	yuġaadiru	يغادر
	muġaadara	مغادرة
To listen	*istamaa*	إستمع
	yastamiu	يستمع
	istimaa	إستماع
To live	*Aaša*	عاش
	yaiišu	يعيش
	maiiša	معيشة
To live in a place	*Sakana*	سكن
	yaskunu	يسكن
	sakan	سكن
To look at	*naZara*	نظر
	yanZuru	ينظر
	naZar	نظر

To look for	*baHata*	بحث
	yabHatu	يبحث
	baHt	بحث
To lose	*Dayyaa*	ضيّع
	yuDayyiu	يضيّع
	taDyii	تضييع
To love	*Habba*	حبّ
	yuHibbu	يحبّ
	Hubb	حبّ
To need	*iHtaaja*	إحتاج
	yaHtaaju	يحتاج
	iHtiyaaj	احتياج
To open	*fataHa*	فتح
	yaftaHu	يفتح
	fatH	فتح
To organize	*naZZama*	نظّم
	yunaZZimu	ينظّم
	tanZiim	تنظيم
To organize	*Rattaba*	رتّب
	yurattibu	يرتّب
	Tartiib	ترتيب

To fail	*Fašila*	فشل
	yafšalu	يفشل
	fašal	فشل
To fall	*waqaa*	وقع
	yaqau	يقع
	wuqu	وقوع
To find	*Wajada*	وجد
	yajidu	يجد
	wujuud	وجود
To finish	*KhallaSa*	خلّص
	yuKhalliSu	يخلّص
	taKhliiS	تخليص
To forget	*Nasiya*	نسي
	yansaa	ينسى
	nasi	نسي
To get up	*Qaama*	قام
	yaquumu	يقوم
	qiyaam	قيام
To give	*aaTa*	أعطى
	yuTi	يعطي
	iTaa'	اعطاء

To pass away	*Tuwuffiya*	توفّي
	yutawaffayu	يتوفي
	wafaah	وفاة
To pay	*dafaa*	دفع
	yadfau	يدفع
	daf	دفع
To play	*laiba*	لعب
	yalabu	يلعب
	laab	لعب
To promise	*waada*	وعد
	yaidu	يعد
	waadu	وعد
To push	*dafaa*	دفع
	yadfau	يدفع
	dafu	دفع
To put	*waDaa*	وضع
	yaDau	يضع
	waDu	وضع
To read	*qara'a*	قرأ
	yaqra'	يقرأ
	qiraa'a	قراءة

To run	*Jara*	جرى
	yajri	يجري
	jary	جري
To say	*Qaala*	قال
	yaquulu	يقول
	qawl	قول
To see	*ra'a*	رأى
	yara	يرى
	ru'ya	رؤية
To sell	*BA'aa*	باع
	yabiu	يبيع
	biih	بيع
To send	*Arsala*	أرسل
	yursilu	يرسل
	irsaal	ارسال
To sit	*Jalasa*	جلس
	yajlisu	يجلس
	juluus	جلوس
To sleep	*Naama*	نام
	yanaamu	ينام
	Nawm	نوم

To receive	*Istalama*	إستلم
	yastalimu	يستلم
	istilaam	إستلام
To remember	*Tadakkara*	تذكر
	yatadakkaru	يتذكر
	tadakkur	تذكر
To reply, answer	*Ajaaba*	أجاب
	yujiibu	يجيب
	ijaabah	إجابة
To reply, answer	*Radda*	ردّ
	yarudd	يردّ
	raddu	ردّ
To request	*Talaba*	طلب
	yaTlubu	يطلب
	Talab	طلب
To return	*rajaa*	رجع
	yarjau	يرجع
	ruju	رجوع
To ride	*Rakiba*	ركب
	yarkabu	يركب
	Rukuub	ركوب

English	Transliteration	Arabic
To smoke	*DaKhaana*	دخّن
	yudaKhinu	يدخّن
	tadKhin	تدخين
To stop	*Waqafa*	وقف
	yaqifu	يقف
	wuquuf	وقوف
To study	*Darasa*	درس
	yadrusu	يدرس
	diraasa	دراسة
To succeed	*najaHa*	نجح
	yanjaHu	ينجح
	najaaH	نجاح
To take	*AKhada*	أخذ
	ya'Khudu	يأخذ
	aKhad	أخذ
To talk reflexive	*Takallama*	تكلّم
	yatakallamu	يتكلّم
	kalaam	تكلّم
To talk reflexive	*taHaddata*	تحدّث
	yataHaddatu	يتحدّث
	taHaddut	تحدّث

To thank	*Šakara*	شكر
	yaškuru	يشكر
	šukr	شكر
To think about	*Fakkara*	فكّر
	yufakkiru	يفكّر
	tafkiir	تفكير
To think that	*Zanna*	ظنّ
	yaZunnu	يظنّ
	Zann anna	ظن أن
To translate	*Tarjama*	ترجم
	yutarjimu	يترجم
	tarjama	ترجمة
To try	*Haawala*	حاول
	yuHaawilu	يحاول
	muHaawala	محاولة
To test	*Jarraba*	جرّب
	yujarribu	يجرّب
	tajriib	تجريب
To understand	*Fahima*	فهم
	yafhamu	يفهم
	Fahm	فهم

To use	IstaKhdama	إستخدم
	yastakhdimu	يستخدم
	istikhdaam	استخدام
To use	istamala	إستعمل
	yastamilu	يستعمل
	istimaal	استعمال
To wait	intaZara	إنتظر
	yantaZiru	ينتظر
	intiZaar	انتظار
To wake up	SaHa	صحى
	yaSHu	يصحو
	SaHw	صحو
To wake up	istayqaZa	إستيقظ
	yastayqiZu	يستيقظ
	istiiqaaZ	استيقاظ
To walk	Maša	مشى
	yamši	يمشي
	mašy	مشي
To want to	Araada	أراد
	yuriidu	يريد
	Iraadah	ارادة

ARABIC

PHRASES

To wash	*Ġasala*	غسل
	yaġsilu	يغسل
	ġasl	غسل
To watch	*Šaahada*	شاهد
	yušaahidu	يشاهد
	mušaahada	مشاهدة
To work	*amala*	عمل
	yamilu	يعمل
	amal	عمل
To write	*Kataba*	كتب
	yaktubu	يكتب
	kitaaba	كتابة

ARABIC PHRASES

Best wishes!

tamaniyaati tayyibati

تمنياتى الطيبة

Bless you (when sneezing)

yarhamuka allah

يرحمك الله

Calm down!

ahada min fazlik

أهدأ من فضلك

Come in

tafazal biddukul

تفضل بالدخول

Come with me!

tafazzal mai'ee

تفضل معى

Don't worry!

laa taqlaq

لا تقلق

Farewell Expressions

ta'abier ul wadaai

تعابير الوداع

Give me this!

aa'tini haza

أعطني هذا

Go straight

imshi fi khatti mustaqeem

امشى فى خط مستقيم

Go to hell!

izhab ilal jaheem

إذهب إلى الجحيم

Good

be khair

بخير

Good

jaiyyid

جيد

Good afternoon!

nahaarukal khair

نهارك الخير

Good bye!

ilal liqaah

إلى اللقاء

Good evening!

masa -al-khair

مساء الخير

Good luck!

hazzun saeed

حظ سعيد

Good morning!

sabaahal khair

صباح الخير

Good night!

lailatun sa'eeda

ليلة سعيدة

Greeting

aatahiyath

التحيات

Happy birthday!

e'id milaad sa'eed

عيد ميلاد سعيد

Have a nice journey!

rihlatan sa'eedatan

رحلة سعيدة

Have a nice day!

ata manna laka nahaaran sa'eedan

أتمنى لك نهارا سعيدا

Hello my friend!

ahlan yaa sadeeqe

أهلا يا صديقى

Help!

saae'dni

ساعدنى

Hi!

ahlan

أهلا

Hot

haar

حار

How are you?

kaifa haalu ka?

كيف حالك ؟

How are you? (friendly)

kaifa haal lu kum?

كيف حالكم ؟

How much is this?

kam saman haza ?

كم ثمن هذا ؟

How old are you?

kam u'murka ?

كم عمرك ؟

Hurry up!

asra'

أسرع

I agree with you

ana muttafiq ma'k

انا متفق معك

I can show you the path!

astatee' an ariika attareeq

أستطيع ان أريك الطريق

laisa ladaiyya fakkah

I don't have change

ليس لدى فكة

I don't know!

laa a'rifu

لا اعرف

I don't understand!

laa afhamu

لا أفهم

I had a good time with you

laqad istamta'tu bilwqti ma'ka jiddan

لقد استمتعت بالوقت معك جدا

I have to go

labudda an arhala

لابد أن أرحل

I just need to practice

ana faqat ahtaju liba'zi attamreen

أنا فقط أحتاج لبعض التمرين

I like Arabic

uhibbu al lugata al a'rabiyata

أحب اللغة العربية

I love you

ana uhibbuka

أنا أحبك

I missed you

laqad iftaqadtuka

لقد افتقدتك

I really like it!

innahu yu'jibuni fa'lan

إنه يعجبني فعلا

I will be back now!

saoofa aaodu haalan

سوف أعود حالا

I will try my best to learn

saufa abzulu qusaara juhudi litta'llum

سوف أبذل قصارى جهدى للتعلم

I would like to invite you to dinner

awaddu an aduaka ila- al a'shaai

أود ان ادعوك إلى العشاء

I would love to visit your country again

uhibbu an azooru bilaadikum saaniya

أحب أن أزور بلادكم ثانية

I'm (twenty) years old

ablugu min al u'mri (e'shroona a'aman)

أبلغ من العمر   عشرون عاما)

I'm fine

ana bi khair

أنا بخير

I'm from

anaa min

أنا من

I'm here on business

ana hina lila'mal

أنا هنا للعمل

I'm hungry

ana jaaiu'n

أنا جائع

I'm just kidding

ana amzahu faqat

أنا أمزح فقط

I'm just looking

ana alqi nazratan faqat

أنا ألقى نظرة فقط

I'm lost

ana taa ih

أنا تائه

I'm married

ana mutazawwijun

انا متزوج

I'm not from here

ana lastu min huna

أنا لست من هنا

I'm serious

ana jaad

أنا جاد

I'm single

ana aa'zib

أنا أعزب

I'm Feeling thirsty

ashu'ru bizzama

أشعر بالظمأ

I'm trying to learn Arabic

uhaawilu ta'llum allugati ala'rabiyati

أحاول تعلم اللغة العربية

I'm very happy

ana sa'eedun jiddan

أنا سعيد جدا

Is this right?

hal haza sahiih ?

هل هذا صحيح ؟

Is this wrong?

hal haza khata ?

هل هذا خطأ ؟

It hurts here

hina yuallimuni

هنا يؤلمنى

It's a hard language

innaha lugatun sa'batun

إنها لغة صعبة

It's an easy language

innaha lugatun sahlatun

إنها لغة سهلة

It's far from here

innaha baee'datun a'n huna

إنها بعيدة عن هنا.

It's freezing (weather)

innal jaw baarid jiddan

إن الجو بارد جدا

It's hot (weather)

innal jaw haar jidda

إن الجو حار جدا

It's near here

innaha qariba min hina

إنها قريبة من هنا.

It's urgent!

innahu amrun haamun

إنه امر هام

Just a little

Qaleel

قليلا

Leave me alone!

utrukni wahdi

أتركني وحدى

Long time no see

lam naraaka munzu waqtin taweel

لم نرك منذ وقت طويل

Look!

unzur

أنظر

Make yourself at home!

tasrraf wa ka annaka fi baitik

تصرف و كأنك فى بيتك

My pleasure

haza min dawae sururi

هذا من دواعى سرورى

My trip was very nice

kaanat rehlatii jaiyyidah

كانت رحلتى جيدة.

Nice to meet you!

sa'eed bi muqaabaltik

سعيد بمقابلتك

Oh! That's good!

fa'lan azeem

فعلا   عظيم

One moment please!

lahza wahda min fazlik

لحظة وحدة من فضلك

Really?

Haqqan ?

حقا ؟

Romance

Romansiyatun

رومانسية

I will send my greetings

arsil tahiyaatee

أرسل تحياتى

See you later!

araaka fi ma ba'd

أراك فيما بعد

See you soon!

araaka qareeban

See you tomorrow!

araaka gadan

أراك قريبا

أراك غدا

Slow

batii

بطئ

Small

sageer

صغير

Sorry

Aasif

آسف

Sorry! (or: I beg your pardon!)

u'zran lam asma'ka jaiyyidan

عذرا لم أسمعك جيدا

Sweet dreams!

ahlaamun asad

أحلام أسعد

So-so

bain bain

بين بين

Stop!

touqaf

توقف

Take this!

tafazzal haza

تفضل هذا

Thank you

shukran (jazeelan)

شكرا   جزيلا)

Then

ba'da zalik

بعد ذلك

Railway station

mahattat ul qitaar

محطة القطار

Turn left

astadir shimaalan

استدر شمالا

Turn right

astadir yameen

استدر يمين

Waiter

naadil

نادل

Welcome!

marhaba

مرحبا

What do you do?

maza ta'mal ?

ماذا تعمل ؟

What should I say?

maaza yajibu an aqoola ?

ما ذا يجب أن أقول ؟

What time is it?

kam issaa' alaan ?

كم الساعة الآن ؟

What's wrong with you?

maa baaluka ?

ما بالك ؟

What's your name?

maa ismak?

ما اسمك ؟

Where are you from?

min aaie balad aanta ?

من أى بلد أنت ؟

Where do you live?

aina taskunu ?

أين تسكن ؟

Wishes

al amaniyath

الأمنيات

Yes

na'm

نعم

Yesterday

amsi

أمس

You are looking beautiful!

tabdi jameelatan

تبدى جميلة!

You will be okay!

saofa takunu bikhair

سوف تكون بخير

Your Arabic is good

lugatuka alarabiya jaiyyidatun

لغتك العربية جيدة

You're welcome!

a'fuwan

عفوا

:: The End ::

www.ingramcontent.com/pod-product-compliance
Lightning Source LLC
LaVergne TN
LVHW041714190726
843493LV00007B/2087